WALKING
THE **DRAMWAY**

WALKING
THE **DRAMWAY**

PETER LAWSON

TEMPUS

First published 2006

Tempus Publishing Limited
The Mill, Brimscombe Port,
Stroud, Gloucestershire, GL5 2QG
www.tempus-publishing.com

British Library Cataloguing in Publication Data.
A catalogue record for this book is available from the British Library.

ISBN 07524 4134 5
  978 07524 4134 4

Typesetting and origination by Tempus Publishing Limited.
Printed in Great Britain.

Contents

A Brief History of the Dramway   7

one   Ram Hill Colliery – Mangotsfield   9

two   Mangotsfield – Warmley   49

three   Warmley – Willsbridge   71

four   Willsbridge – River Avon   93

five   The Dramway – Operation   121

Acknowledgements   126

Bibliography   127

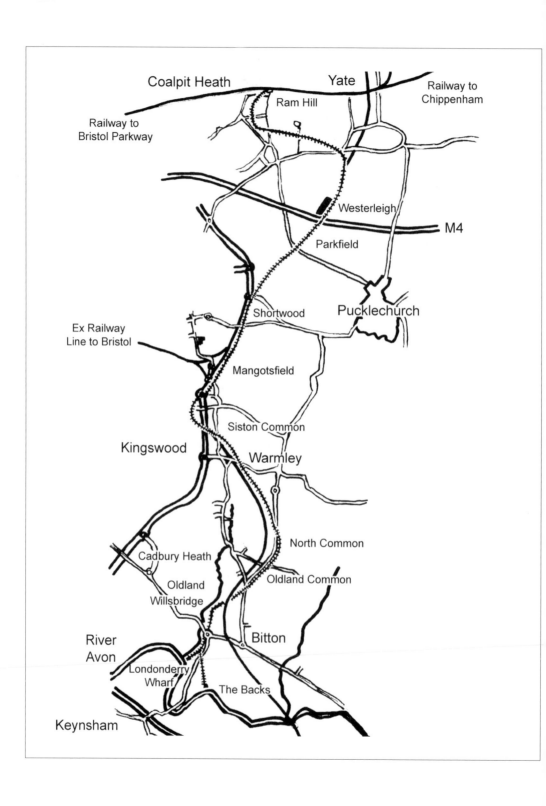

A Brief History of the Dramway

The Dramway was born out of the need to move coal from areas north of Bristol to the heart of the city. After two false starts in 1803 and 1826, a new proposal was put forward for a horse-drawn railway from Orchard Pit in Coalpit Heath to wharfs on the Avon at Keynsham, and Cuckolds Pill in Bristol.

On 19 June 1828 the Bristol & Gloucestershire Railway, which proposed a route between Coalpit Heath & Cuckolds Pill, and the Avon & Gloucestershire Railway, which proposed a route between Shortwood and Avon Wharf in Keynsham, were incorporated into an Act of Parliament.

At the time the Act was obtained the subscribers of the B&GR totalled eighty-five in number and included Sir John Smyth and Sir Henry Nicoll. The B&GR Co. Act gave them the power to raise among themselves the sum of £45,000 in shares of £50 each, and the further power to raise, or to borrow, an additional sum of £12,000.

The subscribers of the A&GR were eleven in number, with the main shareholder being the Kennet & Avon Canal Navigation Co. Of the 210 £100 shares that were made available for purchase, the K&ACNC spent £10,000 on a hundred of them.

Construction work began in 1829, and on 30 July 1831 another Act of Parliament was passed allowing the A&GR to build branches from their main route to other collieries along the line. These branches comprised Bone Mills to Cowhorn Hill Pit at a length of sixty chains; Redfield Lane to Haul Lane Pit at a length of six chains; Crown Inn Warmley to Grimsbury Pit at a length of thirty chains; and Siston Common to Soundwell Pit at a length of forty-three chains. Of these branches, only the ones to Haul Lane (Hole Lane) and Soundwell Pit were actually constructed.

In November 1830 the Dramway transported its first passengers. A train carrying several company managers, who were inspecting the progress of the route, travelled between Avon Wharf and Hole Lane Pit. By the end of December 1830 Hole Lane Pit had sent its first load of coal to Avon Wharf, followed two weeks later by coal from Siston Hill Pit. In 1831 a connection was made to sidings at Shortwood Colliery and coal was flowing from that pit by August.

In 1832 the B&GR route between Bitterwell and Shortwood was finished, and the opening of the line from Shortwood through to Keynsham meant the A&GR was complete. The official opening took place in July of that year. At the end of November 1832, A&GR records show that nearly 3,000 tons of coal had traversed the Dramway that month and that all the railway's wagons were fully employed.

One problem the A&GR had with building a terminus at Keynsham was that coal destined for Bristol had to pass through a set of locks on the river Avon and pay a toll. It was decided to build a branch from Willsbridge to Londonderry Wharf on the Bristol side of the locks. This opened in October 1833, thus completing the Dramway route as described by this book.

Decline and Closure

After the opening of the line between Shortwood and Bristol on 6 August 1835, the B&GR had its mind on expansion and planned an extension northwards towards Gloucester. In 1839, and with the assistance of the GWR, an Act was passed for this new railway, and the Bristol & Gloucester Railway Co. was formed. In April 1843 it was decided that the new railway would be built to broad gauge. The northern section of the Dramway between Shortwood and the junction with Ram Hill Pit was converted during 1844 and, in the process, became the first mixed-gauge track in the country.

With the metamorphosis of the B&GR from a horse-drawn Dramway to a full-blown steam-driven broad-gauge railway, a problem was encountered concerning the safety of running the horse-drawn A&GR traffic along the same section of track as the steam railway. A completely separate narrow-gauge track had been laid inside the broad-gauge railway, but in 1844 an inspection by Captain Codrington of the Board of Trade found the junctions to be unsafe and the quality of the work unsatisfactory. The relationship between the A&GR and the B&GR was said to be hostile. It was recommended that the B&GR should relay the narrow-gauge track with heavier rail or provide for a completely separate railway for the A&GR. The B&GR decided that the cost of such modifications would be more than the traffic was worth, and the coal that flowed from the pits at Coalpit Heath, before the suspension of traffic on 5 June 1844 for the building of the broad-gauge line, proved to be the last from those pits to traverse the Dramway.

The A&GR had seen a marked decline in traffic with the opening of the B&GR in 1835, and by 1843 it is recorded that only about 204 tons of B&GR coal per week were being carried. The loss of the productive pits at Coalpit Heath, and the accompanying closure of many of the pits along its own route due to flooding or exhaustion, meant traffic along the A&GR decreased further.

Under the terms of the Great Western Railway Act No.1, dated 30 June 1852, and by transfer deed dated 29 July 1852, the Kennet & Avon Canal Navigation Co. was taken into the ownership of the GWR. As the K&ACNC owned the A&GR, that passed into GWR ownership at the same time.

Meanwhile, in 1845, the B&GR had been bought by the Midland Railway and in 1864 an Act was passed allowing a branch to be built by the MR from Mangotsfield to Bath. The course of this new railway followed closely that of the Dramway as far as Siston Common, where it then severed the A&GR route in two places. A deviation of the Dramway was built alongside the MR mainline despite the fact that this section of the A&GR had been unused since the conversion of the B&GR to broad gauge some twenty years earlier.

By 5 July 1865 the GWR decided the Dramway was no longer needed and obtained the necessary powers under the GWR (Additional Powers) Act to abandon the route. The final wagon load of coal was sent from Hole Lane Pit in January 1867.

Reprieve

In 1876 Abraham Fussell purchased the Cowhorn Hill and Hole Lane Collieries and founded the Oldland Colliery Co. He deepened an old shaft and renamed it California in the belief that, like the gold prospectors across the Atlantic, he was about to make his fortune.

He needed a way to get his coal to the markets of Bristol and decided to connect his colliery with the Dramway, which lay across Willsbridge Valley on the other side of Siston Brook. Undeterred by the terrain, Fussell built a new branch of the Dramway and routed it from his colliery down a 1 in 10 incline, across Siston Brook on a bridge, and connected it via a new trailing junction with the main A&GR route. The junction was built so that any runaways on the incline would be diverted uphill where they would come to a natural halt, rather than careering downhill out of control in the direction of Willsbridge.

The Dramway itself had been repaired at the expense of the colliery and a new land wharf was built at Willsbridge to supply local markets with California Colliery coal. The necessary works required to reopen the Dramway were completed in 1881.

The End

In March 1904 a tremendous flood burst through the workings of California Colliery and miners barely escaped with their lives. This catastrophe bankrupted the Oldland Colliery Co. and the pit closed.

On 9 July 1906 the GWR Traffic Committee was informed that all traffic along the route had ceased and the Dramway officially closed, never to reopen.

one

Ram Hill Colliery – Mangotsfield

Of all the pits in this part of Coalpit Heath, Ram Hill was one of the last to be sunk, probably some time between 1820 and 1830. It was owned by the Coalpit Heath Co., which included Sir John Smyth as a shareholder. Sir John was one of the main proponents of the Bristol & Gloucestershire Railway.

Ram Hill was 558ft deep and was originally worked by a horse gin, the remains of which are still visible. In later years it was worked by a beam winding engine. The pit was linked underground to Churchlease, New Engine and Rose Oak Pits.

Published records state that the section of Dramway between Westerleigh Junction and the Coalpit Heath collieries was converted to broad gauge for use by steam engines during 1847. The remains of the Dramway between Ram Hill and Bitterwell Lake clearly show that this section was not converted.

A tragic accident occurred at the pit in October 1855 when Job Dando and George Ralph were killed after the rope hauling their cage to the surface broke.

Abandonment plans show that the colliery, along with other Coalpit Heath pits at Churchlease and New Engine, closed in the 1860s as the nearby Frog Lane Colliery increased production. In later years the area was purchased by the GWR for the construction of their direct route to South Wales via Badminton and, although their line passed through the area in a deep cutting, the works stopped short just to the north of the pit.

The site was rediscovered by local archaeologist and author John Cornwell in 1981 and has since been excavated, first by workers on a job creation scheme, and latterly by the 'Friends of Ram Hill Colliery'.

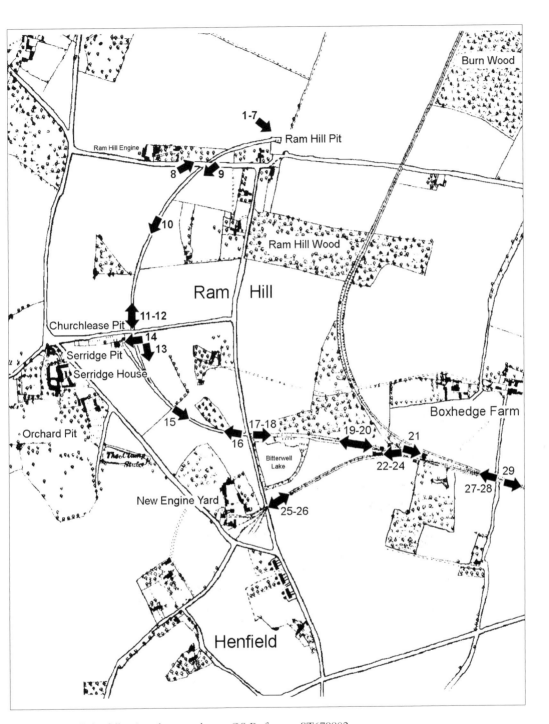

Above: All the following photographs are OS Reference ST679802.

1 Opposite: The terminus of the Dramway at Ram Hill Pit. The houses in the background were built by the GWR. The Bristol Parkway to Swindon mainline passes just a few yards from the site of the colliery.

2 The section of the Dramway between the Coalpit Heath Collieries and Westerleigh Junction was converted to broad gauge during 1847 at a cost of £1,450. The remains here, and further south to Bitterwell Lake, clearly show that the branch to Ram Hill was not converted.

3 The oval shaft of the pit. Unfortunately a boundary fence goes right across the middle of it.

4 The remains of the horse gin. The walls suggest that the structure was covered with a roof.

5 The next three photographs show the remains of the beam engine.

6 & 7 Left and below: Ram Hill Colliery
– Bitterwell Lake.

8 Opposite top: The remains of the
Dramway form a small embankment
across a paddock. The approach road to
the site of Coalpit Heath station is out of
sight on the left.

9 Above: After crossing Ram Hill, this route has been utilised as an access road.

10 Right: The Bristol & Gloucestershire Railway bought some blocks from a quarry belonging to the Avon & Gloucestershire Railway. These were delivered to them at Rodway Junction at a price of 1*s* per 16in square block, and 1*s* 8*d* per 20in square block.

11 The Dramway route continues around the back of Coalpit Heath Cricket Club.

12 The route then crosses Serridge Lane.

13 The view towards Bitterwell Lake from the stile at Serridge Lane. The Dramway has long been ploughed into oblivion at this spot.

14 This was the site of Churchlease Pit. Serridge Pit, which had an engine erected by William Bond and Thomas Palmer in 1790, was on the spot where the houses in the distance now stand. Both pits closed in the 1860s when Frog Lane Colliery increased production.

15 The route then crosses a field before re-crossing Ram Hill. The hedge from behind which this photograph was taken is one of the best spots to pick blackberries for miles around.

16 Just before the trackbed reaches Ram Hill it becomes an access route to a farm building.

Bitterwell Lake – Westerleigh

17 After crossing Ram Hill the Dramway passes the north side of Bitterwell Lake. The official Dramway Footpath takes a deviation of a couple of miles from the trackbed at this point, not rejoining the route until south of the M4 motorway.

18 The car park at Bitterwell Lake. The route of the Dramway is marked by the hedge at the left of this photograph. The lake itself was created to provide a reservoir of water for the colliery engines, and to soak pit props before they were used underground. It is now used for fishing.

19 Once past Bitterwell Lake, the route of the Dramway becomes a linear scrap yard.

20 This whole section of the route is very atmospheric. Some of the vehicles are of Second World War vintage.

21 The scrap yard was the site of two junctions; a branch to Frog Lane Pit and another to New Engine Pit. The branch to Frog Lane was built in the 1860s after the Bristol & Gloucester Railway had been taken over by the Midland Railway.

22 Just visible under a carpet of ivy is an abandoned engine house. This was home to several small steam engines that worked the branch to Frog Lane. One engine, a 1906 Peckett 0-6-0 inside-cylindered Saddle Tank named *Lord Salisbury*, ended her days at the Norton Hill Colliery near Midsomer Norton before being scrapped in Trowbridge in 1965.

23   Inside the building an old fireplace is visible. The remains of an ivy-clad egg-ended boiler sit on top of a chimney. The boiler came from New Engine Pit and was reused as a water tank for the Frog Lane Colliery locomotives. Other engines that worked the Frog Lane branch included a Peckett 0-6-0ST works No.825 *Lord Roberts*, and Fox, Walker Works No.326, another 0-6-0ST.

24   This view looks out through the dilapidated doors. There is a rubble-filled pit in the floor here. The branch to Frog Lane Colliery closed in 1949, but a section remained in use until 1956 as storage for redundant wagons.

25 The branch to New Engine Pit crossed Ram Hill south of Bitterwell Lake.

26 A path follows the route of the Dramway. New Engine was the main Coalpit Heath Co. colliery for many years, and was operational after Ram Hill had closed. When Frog Lane Colliery opened, New Engine became a workshop and wood yard.

27 *Opposite above:* This abandoned building in the scrap yard was a weighbridge house. A milepost once stood opposite marking the end of Midland Railway territory.

28 *Opposite below:* The view from Boxhedge Farm Lane back towards Bitterwell Lake. At the time of writing the route is being cleared.

29 The route continues across this part of the path from Boxhedge Farm Lane in a broad arc to Kidney Hill. There is a gate with a padlock and so it cannot be walked without the permission of the landowner.

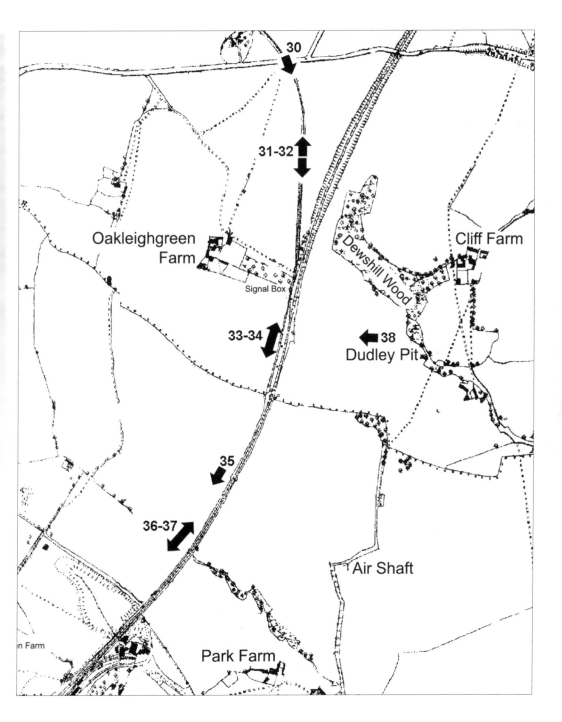

30 Opposite above: At Kidney Hill the route of the Dramway has become a road which is now also redundant.

31 Opposite below: The route then becomes an access road leading to Westerleigh Oil Terminal.

32 Looking south towards Westerleigh Sidings. This was the site of Westerleigh Junction and the spot from where Bristol & Gloucester Railway built a railway northwards. From here through to Mangotsfield the Dramway route was swallowed up by the building of the B&GR in 1844.

33 The view north. The C2 board defines the limit of the present-day Westerleigh yard. Any train that enters the section of track beyond the board can only do so on the authority of the Bristol Signal Box.

34 A footpath crosses the railway and a level crossing leads to Westerleigh Training Centre. The supervisor at the centre is in charge of the yard when on duty, and is responsible for authorising train movements into the yard and the Training Centre Sidings. The centre is used to train people in the use of permanent way vehicles.

35 56055 stands at the head of a train being loaded at Avon County Council's Westerleigh refuse transfer station. The depot was built on the site of Westerleigh Up Sidings and opened on 19 November 1985.

36 The route of the Dramway then passes Murco's Westerleigh Oil Terminal which opened for business on 1 March 1991. This view north was taken from the top of one of the distillate tanks.

37 Looking south along the route of the Dramway from Westerleigh Oil Terminal. The M4 crosses the railway on a bridge, and the railway underneath the motorway is used as a garage for permanent way vehicles. The chimney in the background belongs to Parkfield Colliery.

38 There is an old colliery tramway in a field east of Westerleigh Oil Depot. It leads up the hillside to the long abandoned Dudley Colliery. All published maps that I have seen show this tramway connecting with the mainline in a northerly direction, while the earthworks clearly show that it connected in a southerly direction. The shaft at Dudley Colliery was said to be 345ft deep.

39 Miner's cottages at Parkfield.

Parkfield Colliery

Parkfield Colliery was sunk in 1851 under the ownership of Handel Cossham, who employed men from Staffordshire to do the sinking. Coal was reached in 1853. The shaft was 840ft deep, but only the upper series of coal veins were worked. These were the Hard, the Top, the Hollybush and the Great veins. The quality of the coal mined was extremely good, and was used for gas manufacture and house coal.

When Handel Cossham died in 1890 the pit was put up for sale (along with other pits he had owned at Deep Pit, South Pit and Speedwell). It was purchased by Bristol United Collieries, owners of Dean Lane, Easton, Hanham, Pennywell Road and Whitehall collieries. They formed a new company to manage their assets called The Bedminster, Easton, Kingswood and Parkfield Collieries Ltd.

A survey of Parkfield Colliery at the time of sale noted that it had two horizontal direct-acting steam winding engines, each with 28in cylinders, a 4ft stroke and a drum 15ft in diameter. These had been made by Teague & Chew of Cinderford in the Forest of Dean. There were two 38ft-high headgears, each with two pulley wheels of 15ft diameter. Steam was provided by four Lancashire boilers which measured 27ft by 7ft. A ventilating fan measured 18ft by 7ft and was driven by a pair of horizontal engines which had 14in cylinders and a 16in stroke. A Cornish pumping engine had a 54in cylinder and a 7ft stroke and was powered by two Lancashire boilers.

The pit had an endless haulage system comprising a beam engine and two galvanised ropes, each 990ft in length. Underground there were three engines for haulage, 5,250ft of single T-headed rails, 4,350ft of bridge rails and 5,400ft of tram bridge rails.

The 1896 'List of Mines worked under the Coal Mines Regulation Act' states that the colliery employed 292 people underground and forty-nine people on the surface. The manager was J.T. Onions and the under-manager was John Bullough.

In 1914 Parkfield was bought by Frank Beauchamp, owner of a number of collieries in the Radstock area, and another company, East Bristol Collieries Ltd, was formed.

By 1936 flooding was becoming problematic and this combined with increasing pumping costs and decreasing coal reserves resulted in the pit becoming uneconomic. It closed on 15 August of that year.

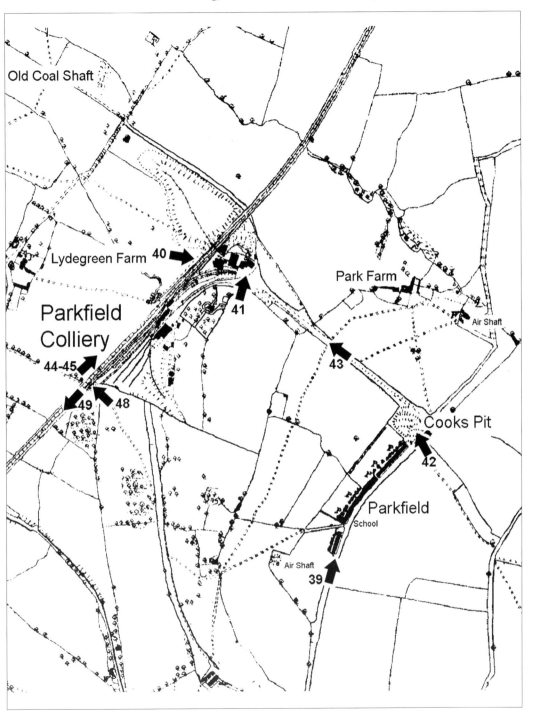

Old Coal Shaft

Lydegreen Farm **40**

Park Farm

Air Shaft

Parkfield Colliery

44-45

41

43

49 48

Cooks Pit

42

Parkfield

School

Air Shaft

39

40 Opposite below: Some remains of a building at Parkfield with the colliery chimney (a landmark from the nearby motorway) behind it.

41 The army once made an offer to blow up the chimney as part of a training exercise but, because the remaining rubble would have been on private land, they would not have been able to take it away. Their offer was consequently turned down.

42 Opposite above: At the top of the hill on Parkfield Road is the site of Cooks Pit. This was used by Handel Cossham for the extraction of coal while Parkfield Colliery was being sunk, and was the scene of a gruesome death in 1860. Fifty-year-old William King was hauling water out from the pit at 12.30 a.m. and Charles Lacey was working the engine. The cage should have been level with the top of the pit in order to stop anything from falling down the shaft, but Lacey had not applied the brake and the cage moved 3½ft above the shaft. King did not notice that the cage had moved and thus fell down the shaft, colliding with another cage at the bottom which severed the top part of his head. An inquest jury questioned whether a case of manslaughter could be brought against Lacey but, after hearing that it was not customary to apply the brake when the cage was in the ketches, and that he had exemplary references, a verdict of accidental death was brought in. King, a widower, left six children.

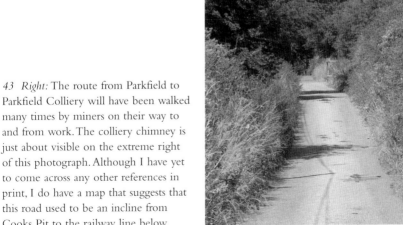

43 Right: The route from Parkfield to Parkfield Colliery will have been walked many times by miners on their way to and from work. The colliery chimney is just about visible on the extreme right of this photograph. Although I have yet to come across any other references in print, I do have a map that suggests that this road used to be an incline from Cooks Pit to the railway line below.

44 Above: An 1876 view of the north, showing the railway sidings and timber yard.

45 Below: The view north. At one time the pit was home to a formidable football team formed from eleven brothers of the Hunt family.

Brandy Bottom Colliery

Brandy Bottom Pit was one of the oldest collieries in the area. It was sunk in the late 1790s/early 1800s and owned by Lord Radnor. Between the 1850s and 1870s Jefferies, Walters & Co. worked the pit.

Tragedy struck Brandy Bottom on 3 February 1853 when a falling rafter knocked Isaac Bryant into one of the pit engines. He left a widow and six children. Another inquest held on 25 November 1856 tells of the death of William Strange of Pucklechurch, while a further death occurred in 1868 when Thomas Woodington of Siston was killed. His inquest was held on 4 February 1868.

In 1871 Handel Cossham acquired Brandy Bottom. (He had sunk Parkfield Pit just to the north in 1851.) As the new owner, Cossham sank a second shaft 618ft deep and called it 'New Pit'.

By the time the 1896 'List of Mines worked under the Coal Mines Regulation Act' was published, Brandy Bottom had become known as South Pit. The inspector, Joseph S. Martin, recorded that there were 155 men working underground and seventeen men working on the surface. The manager was J. Sparkes Jnr and the under-manager R. Nicholls.

By 1899, as Parkfield expanded, all coal was extracted from the northern pithead, while Brandy Bottom was retained only for pumping and ventilation.

Handel Cossham died in 1890 and his pits were put up for sale. A survey at the time reported that Brandy Bottom had a Cornish engine with a 60in cylinder and 8ft stroke that was powered by two Lancashire boilers 27ft long and 7ft in diameter. The horizontal winding engine had an 8ft flywheel, 12in cylinders and an 18in stroke. This lifted two cast-iron cages. The headgear had two pulley wheels each 7ft in diameter.

When Parkfield Colliery closed in 1936, Brandy Bottom closed with it. Since closure Brandy Bottom has become a Scheduled Ancient Monument and any work to maintain the area requires the permission of the Secretary of State as well as, or instead of, planning permission. In 2003 it was added to English Heritage's endangered building list.

At the time of writing, Brandy Bottom is owned by Ibstock and the buildings are the subject of a scheme of repair and renovation under the Landfill Tax Credit Scheme. The project is managed by Avon Industrial Buildings.

46 The remains of Brandy Bottom Pit.

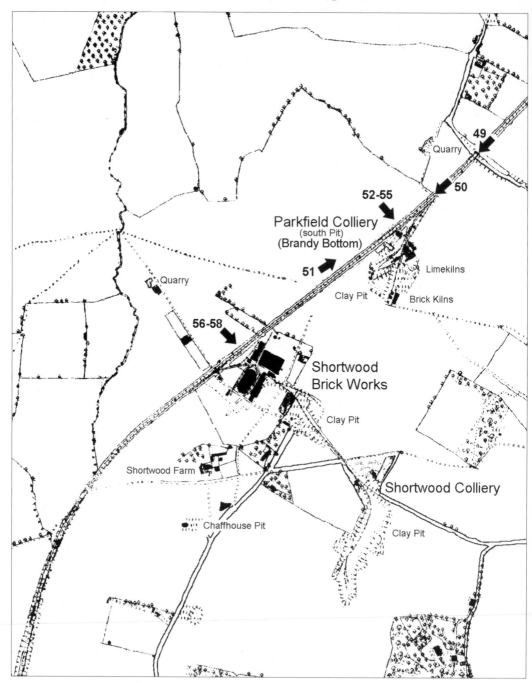

47 *Opposite above:* After taking a detour of a mile and a half, the official Dramway footpath regains the route just south of the site of Parkfield Colliery.

48 *Opposite below:* The view south.

49 The view south from the railway bridge at Coxgrove Hill. The chimney of Brandy Bottom Pit dominates the scene.

50 The remains of an old winding wheel have been placed alongside the cyclepath.

51 *Above:* A 1980s view north from the Dramway route.

52 *Right:* A closer look at the strange octagonal top of the chimney. It is in desperate need of repair.

53 The remains of a Cornish engine house are slowly disintegrating as weeds take over the colliery site.

54 These derelict remains, and the bottom part of the chimney, are built in White Lias stone, whereas the top section of the chimney and other works at the colliery are in brick. This shows that the pit had two distinct phases during its working life.

55 The horizontal engine house at Brandy Bottom.

Shortwood Colliery

The Shortwood Collieries comprised a number of early pits and were centred on the area near Shortwood Brick and Tile works. The pits in this area include Upper and Lower Wood Pits, Chaffhouse Pit (known as Shortwood Pit), Cook's Pit, Thatcher Pit and Lapwater Pit. Lapwater Pit was originally known as Shortwood Lower Pit.

Shortwood Pit was connected to the Dramway in 1831. The A&GR had originally intended to build the branch to the colliery but, after complaints from the B&GR about the A&GR's plan to construct a branch to Londonderry Wharf, it was agreed that the B&GR would build the route instead.

In 1833 the pits were being worked by Messrs Waters and Reynolds who were charged £6 1s by the A&GR for hire of wagons. In 1841 they employed 120 people, fifty of whom were children. The under-manager was Charles James who was forty-seven years old. By 1854 the pits were under the ownership of Handel Cossham.

An inquest held on 14 June 1855 tells how coalminer Job Rich of Mangotsfield was killed by a roof fall at the colliery. He was sixty-four years old.

In the 1896 'List of Mines worked under the Coal Mines Regulation Act', Shortwood Pit is listed as being in the ownership of the Shortwood Colliery Co. There were twenty-seven people working underground and five on the surface. Coal worked was in the Hard Vein. Other coal seams worked at the Shortwood collieries were the Top Vein, the Hollybush Vein and the Great Vein.

In 1908 the Navarra Coal and Iron Mines Ltd owned Shortwood Pit. They closed it in October of that year at a time when it employed 102 workers below ground and eleven above. The manager of the pit at that time was T. Mayberry and the under-manager was F. Kirby.

Shortwood Brickworks

56 A view of Shortwood Brickworks from the trackbed of the Dramway. At the rear of the buildings a narrow-gauge railway connected a quarry to the brickworks. The clay produced bricks that were famous for their exceptional strength.

57 The brickworks was taken over by Cattybrook in 1904 and again by Ibstock in 1972. Manufacturing ceased in 1969 although clay was still extracted for use at the Cattybrook works near Almondsbury. The buildings were demolished in 2000.

58 The manager's house and one of the chimneys at the brickworks.

59 A 1980s view north from the derelict railway route showing the bridge across the railway at Pomphrey Hill.

60 Almost immediately after Pomphrey Hill the route of the Dramway passes the original 1845 B&GR Mangotsfield station.

61 Mangotsfield station, this time pictured in 2005. It has been restored beautifully, but has a dual-carriageway for a neighbour. The station closed in 1869 with the opening of a new Mangotsfield station on the Midland Railway's route between Bristol and Bath.

62 This section of the house is an old A&GR tollhouse. This was built in 1830 and cost £100 to erect. It was fitted with a Foster, Rastrick & Co. weighing machine which cost £95 6*d*. Wagons that were about to traverse the next section of the Dramway were weighed here before continuing their journey to Keynsham.

63 A 1980s photograph of the remains of Mangotsfield North Junction. The B&GR's route to Cuckolds Pill diverged to the right, while the A&GR's route went straight ahead, although the trackbed in this shot is that of the Midland Railway's route to Bath. The building just visible in the centre of the photograph belonged to Carsons Chocolates and Confectionery Ltd. Completed in 1913, it was built using bricks from Shortwood Brickworks. The factory was demolished in 1998 and the land used for a housing estate.

64 Just past Mangotsfield station is a recreation of the Dramway using stone sleepers and fish-bellied rail.

two

Mangotsfield –
Warmley

Soundwell Colliery

The Soundwell Collieries were sunk by Samuel Whittuck & Co. and consisted of Upper Pit, Middle Pit and Lower Pit. Upper Pit was in Gladstone Street and was 1,194ft deep. Middle Pit was located on the junction of Gladstone Street and Church Road and was also 1,194ft deep. This pit spanned Gladstone Road with the shaft on the north side and the winding house on the south. Lower Pit was on Chiphouse Road. It comprised both a winding and pumping shaft and was 1,080ft deep. It was the oldest of the Soundwell collieries with the earliest recorded date being a 1750 invoice for the installation of a Newcommen pump.

Surviving records of the early years at Soundwell Pit reveal an appalling safety record. In June 1794 fourteen-year-old William Bryant fell into the shaft and died, while a year later thirteen-year-old Abraham Bayley died the same way. In August 1795 George Woodington, a forty-five-year-old Bitton man, plunged to his death when the rope attached to his cage broke. On 13 April 1796 an inquest at Bitton heard of the death of sixteen-year-old George Crew, another boy to fall down the shaft at the pit. Henry Garland was killed when he fell from the tip of the pit to the bottom. Death occurred about five hours afterwards. His inquest took place at Soundwell on 22 June 1798.

In 1801 Samuel Whittuck inherited his father's collieries. Wages at that time were 10s a week for men while boys earned between 4d and 6d a day.

More deaths occurred at the pit in 1803. John Poole was killed in February while using gunpowder to blow up part of the colliery, and George Bryant and Samuel Peacock were killed in August when the rope attached to their cage broke 15ft from the bottom of the shaft.

Eighteen-year-old Joseph Flook was killed in February 1809 when 2 tons of stone fell on him. His inquest took place on 16 February and he was buried on the 19th. Later that year a possible relation, fourteen-year-old William Flook, was killed when a large stone fell on his head while he descended the shaft.

A most gruesome event took place in December 1814. Samuel Garland was killed when a steam engine severed his head from his body.

In 1821 both Daniel Bennett, the son of John Bennett, and Daniel Bennett, the son of George Bennett, were drowned in the reservoir of the shaft when they fell out of the cage while ascending. Four others escaped unhurt. The father of one of the children, George Bennett, was killed at the pit in 1829. He plunged 78ft to the bottom of the shaft when yet another winding rope broke. It was said he lived for half an hour after the fall.

In January 1831 Samuel Whittuck proposed a connection from Lower Pit to the Dramway and offered to pay £450 to the A&GR if they would build the line. The A&GR responded that they were not in a position to build the line at that time, but if he could build the line himself they would assist by letting him use the railway and its wagons free of charge. The Bill for construction of the branch was passed by Parliament on 30 July 1831.

By October 1831 the branch was complete enough for the colliery to send coal south. The accounts for that month show that the rails and chairs for the branch had cost £276 5s 8d and the formation of the railway had cost £80 11s 11d. The wages paid amounted to £163 0s 6d, and the men had drunk £4 5s 7d worth of beer. The final cost of the branch was £716 13s 4d. The A&GR paid for the construction of the line and the colliery paid them back the money in instalments of £234.

The Children's Employment Commission report of 4 June 1841 has an interesting section devoted to the pit. The inspector, Elijah Waring, notes that on his visit he failed to find the manager present, so instead talked to a collier in the yard. He learned that there were about twenty boys aged thirteen and under at the pit. They were employed as carters and earned between 2s and 7s a week.

Waring described most of the boys at the pit as 'very stupid and uncouth, even more so than common among their class. Their appearance was healthy, after the underground fashion, and they ran as lightly as bucks, on their road home'.

Two boys whom Waring talked to were fourteen-year-old William Beese and his twelve-year-old brother George. They hauled coal six yards along a 4ft passage and earned 6d a day. Both were described as having good appetites, as generally having enough to eat, but who sometimes went hungry. Both boys could read and attended Sunday school.

Waring also talked to Daniel Poole, aged fifty. He had been a collier all his life and earned 13*s* a week cutting coal at the face. He was in good health and was learning to read at the Moravian Sunday school in Kingswood. Poole was a father of nine children and said it was hard to look after them because provisions were costly. He would have liked to send them to Sunday school, but he could not because they did not have any decent clothes to wear.

Tragedy occurred at Upper Pit in 1845. Thomas Bird, William Bassett, Ben Wiltshire and John Porter were all killed after the rope hauling them to the surface broke and they fell down the shaft.

A further accident occurred in December 1851. The boiler of the winding engine exploded while lowering a cart of timber, and Thomas Waller was killed while attending the resultant fire. Francis Fowler was severely scalded and taken to the Bristol Royal Infirmary.

Perhaps the last accident to occur at the pit took place in December 1852. John Green was killed while loading a 2-ton bucket suspended from a rope. The rope snapped and the bucket fell on his head, killing him. His inquest heard that it was eight hours before his body could be brought to the surface.

The Soundwell collieries closed in 1853 when miners disturbed the remains of the nearby Lodge Pits and water broke through, overloading the pumps and flooding the workings. The pits were put up for sale, and the Mining Journal of 1860 carried an advert for the disposal of the colliery engines.

Mangotsfield – Siston Common

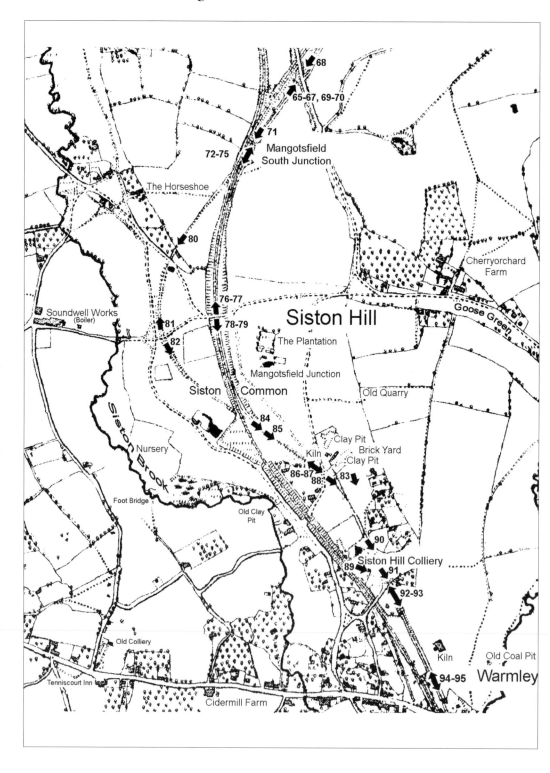

65 The route of the Dramway passes under Carsons Road. This photograph shows the Midland Railway
bridge with the A&GR tunnel next to it.

66 In 1999, work began on the construction of the Avon Ring Road which was built on the Midland Railway trackbed. This involved building a new bridge to carry Carsons Road across the route of the dual-carriageway, and the demolition of the railway bridge. Fortunately, the Dramway tunnel was preserved.

67 The Dramway tunnel was protected by metal shuttering to prevent any accidental damage from equipment used during the construction of the road.

68 Above: The restored Dramway tunnel as viewed from the north. The dual-carriageway is inches away to the right of the photograph.

69 Left: The view north shows the bridge that was constructed to take Carsons Road across the dual-carriageway.

70 Above: The route at this spot is commemorated by this lovely marker.

71 Below: The next structure along the line is the Ghost Bridge. It got its name when the Midland Railway built a route through the area and the lane across the top of the bridge was closed. For many years the bridge stood buried in thick undergrowth, going nowhere and with nothing underneath it.

72 Opposite above: The view north. The bridge at Carsons Road is just visible through the arch.

73 Opposite below: This bridge has also had a marker placed alongside.

74 *Above:* This view looks south. Beyond the gate the route comes to an abrupt halt at the Avon Ring Road roundabout on Siston Common.

75 *Left:* This photograph was taken on what is now the centre of the roundabout. This is the view south. The Dramway route was intersected by the Midland Railway during the construction of its route to Bath. Despite the Dramway having lain unused for over twenty years, and because there was insufficient height between the two routes to build a bridge, a diversion was built alongside the Midland Railway.

76 *Opposite above:* A 1980s view north from the bridge at Siston Hill showing the Midland Railway route after conversion to a cyclepath by Sustrans in the early 1980s.

77 *Opposite below:* Believe it or not, this is the same view north from Siston Hill. The bridge where the previous photograph was taken was demolished during the construction of the dual-carriageway. The roundabout in the distance is where the Midland Railway route and the Dramway crossed.

78 A 1980s view south from the same spot.

79 Using great skill and judgement, local councillors decided to destroy the possibility of restoring a railway route between Bristol and Bath which, unlike the neighbouring Great Western Railway route, travels through some of the most densely populated areas of Bristol. In the process they destroyed a level cyclepath and replaced it with one on an incline, ruined a large chunk of Siston Common, and increased noise and pollution levels.

80 The next three photographs show the section of the Dramway that was abandoned when the Midland Railway built their line to Bath. At Siston Common a cottage occupied by William Packer, and owned by Phillipa Toghill and Thomas Peckstone Peterson, was rebuilt at a cost of £119 to allow the Dramway to pass. Toghill & Peterson owned a lot of land in Siston, including land bought from them for the construction of the Dramway branch to Soundwell Colliery.

81 The view south from Siston Hill. The Dramway survey map of 1827 shows two collieries at this location, one each side of the route. The low building in the foreground is thought to have been an old winding house. It was converted at an early date into a cider press. The Horseshoe pub, just out of view at the left of the photograph, supplied beer to the men building the Soundwell branch of the Dramway. The branch followed an alignment to the left of the main route and passed in front of the pub.

Siston Hill Colliery

The sinking date for Siston Hill is unknown. However, an inquest into the deaths at the pit of ten-year-old Francis Batman and eight-year-old Sampson Brain is dated 14 September 1798. The two lads were killed after 'letting go of the rope' while descending the shaft. Francis died at once while Sampson lived for fourteen hours after the accident. The inquest was held at The Horseshoe Inn, Siston.

Another inquest at the Horseshoe Inn on 25 June 1804 names a Mrs Peterson as the owner of the pit. The inquest heard how twenty-two-year-old Joseph Price was killed after 6 tons of rock fell on him. An inquest on 28 November 1809 names a Mr Toghill as the colliery owner. It is likely that this was in partnership with the aforementioned Mrs Peterson. The inquest heard how twelve-year-old John Lewis of Siston was killed when a large stone fell on his head. John was buried in Siston on 31 December.

The first coal from Siston Hill to traverse the Dramway was sent on 16 January 1831. In June and August 1832, the Toghills sold some of their land and a cottage to the A&GR. The land was used to build the branch to Soundwell Colliery.

Another accident occurred under Toghill & Co.'s ownership on 6 August 1836 when Thomas Jefferis was killed by a roof fall. The inquest into his death states that his body was so mutilated that the remains were carried away in a sack.

On 17 October 1874 the colliery manager, a Mr Henry Gay, was awarded a First Class Certificate of Service as a Manager of Mines granted under the Coal Mines Regulation Act, 1872. Henry was forty-one years old and married to Sarah Jane. They had six children, the oldest being fifteen years old, the youngest ten.

Another accident occurred at the pit in 1876. Albert Haskins, who was thirty-three years old, was killed after falling down an old shaft. Another miner, George Snailham, discovered Haskins lying on his back saying he was going to die. The inquest took place on 16 May.

The 1880 List of Mines names the owner of the pit as S.H. Hadley.

The pit was put up for sale in 1889 and the prospectus states that it had four shafts, two of which were sunk to a depth of 570ft. The winding shaft was 9ft in diameter, walled throughout and had two separate cages. The winding engine was a Boulton and Watt, had a 4ft 6in stroke, a 12ft drum and could lift 700 to 800 tons of coal a day. The pumping engine had two 19in cylinders and was in working order. Above ground was a bank high enough for double screens which sorted the coal before it was loaded for transportation. Drams from the pit were weighed at the top of the bank, while wagons on the Dramway were weighed on a separate weighbridge at the bottom. A tunnel was provided at the bottom of the bank to enable timber and other materials to descend into the pit without first being hauled to the top. A 100ft-high circular chimney stack towered over the colliery.

The sale was not a success and the colliery never reopened. Henry Gay, the colliery manager in 1874 was still alive on the 1901 census. He was a colliery manager living on Court Road in Kingswood.

82 Opposite above: The view north from the same spot shows an area of Siston Common known as the Warrens.

83 Opposite below: Siston Hill Colliery as sketched in the early 1900s by the renowned Bristol artist Samuel Loxton.

Siston Common – Warmley

84 The official Dramway footpath rejoins the trackbed after a diversion through a tunnel under the ring road.

85 The footpath then crosses Siston Common on an embankment.

86 The Dramway originally crossed Siston Hill by means of a bridge, but the crossing is now on the level. Stonework from the bridge was discovered during maintenance work on the road in the early 1980s.

87 The view north. The boulder helps protect the Dramway from illegal parking.

88 The Dramway crosses Siston Common and heads in the direction of Norman Road. The area to the left of this photograph was once a clay pit and brick yard. The area to the right and in the background is the site of Siston Hill Colliery.

89 A view of one of the capped shafts of Siston Hill Pit. The concrete cap is inscribed NCB 1.8.50.

90 The Dramway then passes under Norman Road. The bridge was built in 1830 and follows the same design as used by the Kennet & Avon Canal Co. on their waterway.

91 The barrier is made from rail, but of a modern design and is not a relic of the Dramway.

92 The bridge viewed from the other side.

93 Looking south beyond Norman Road. This section of the route can be very overgrown and muddy.

94 The land between Norman Road and the railway station at Warmley was the site of the Hollybrook Brick Co. In the 1880s, the owner, a Mr Coslett, negotiated the repair of the Dramway from Warmley to the river Avon. However, the traffic generated amounted to nothing, with receipts not paying half the interest on the debt incurred by repairing the line. This is the view south with the chimney of Crown Colliery, and the spire of St Barnabas church, visible in the distance.

95 In 1936 the brickworks was acquired by a firm of accountants, Morgan Brothers & Co. who renamed it the Hollychrome Brick & Tile Co. Ltd. This company was bought in 1964 by a Sheffield firm, the Hepworth Iron Co. Production ceased in the early 1970s.

96 The view north from Warmley High Street.

97 The Dramway route south has been built on, and a small diversion is required to continue following its path.

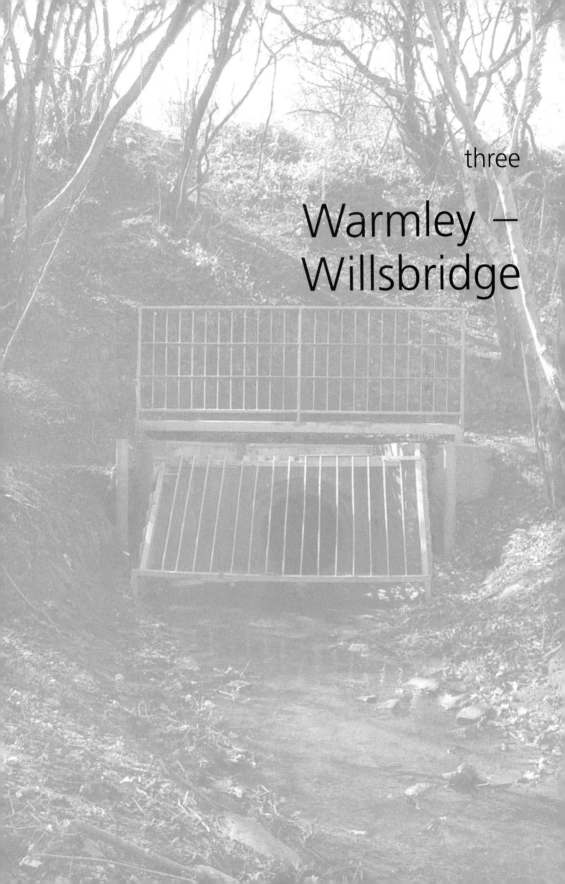

three

Warmley –
Willsbridge

Crown Colliery

098 A 1970s view of the remains of Crown Colliery, showing the engine house and chimney stack, erected in 1900.

The remains of Crown Colliery are still visible on both sides of the A420 road near Warmley station on the closed Midland Railway route between Mangotsfield and Bath. An engine house survives, albeit in a much rebuilt condition, and on the opposite side of the road are buildings thought to have been the blacksmith's shop.

The sinking date of the colliery is unknown, but certainly occurred before 1828 when it appeared on the schedule of land to be acquired for the building of the Dramway. The land was owned by Dr Edwin Woodward and the colliery was worked by Davidson & Co. The Dramway was originally routed straight through the pit, but deviations surveyed in 1829 took it on a straighter course to the west.

The pumping shaft at the pit was 504ft deep and had a 50hp engine, while the winding shaft was 480ft deep and had a 22hp engine. The rope was plaited and there was a running stage over the pit to help prevent accidents. Ventilation was said to be good except when the wind was blowing against the pit's mouth, which could cause a build-up of noxious gas. The seams worked were 2ft 2in wide and the strata dipped to the east by 1ft in 25.

In 1839 there was an inquest into a death at the colliery. A man had apparently gone to an old part of the pit for warmth, the workings being out of the way of the draught blowing through other parts of the pit. He fell asleep and was killed when the roof collapsed and suffocated him.

On 17 May 1841 the pit was visited by Elijah Waring as part of his work for the Children's Employment Commission report of 1842. He conducted an in-depth review of the working conditions at the colliery, and spoke at length to Mr Thomas Waters, the managing partner. Mr Waters reported that the pit employed sixty hands, eleven of whom were under thirteen, the youngest being nine. The wages of the boys varied from 2s 6d to 10s a week, depending on how

99 A 2006 view of the engine house. This has been rebuilt and extended and the chimney stack demolished.

much experience they had and how many hours they worked. The jobs they did included repairing the roads and carrying pit timbers as well as hauling coal in skips. The wages were paid on the Saturday of each week.

Mr Waring's report is a damning portrayal of conditions at the pit. He found evidence of the older boys bullying the younger ones into doing more than their fair share of the work, and of boys working while hungry. In one case a boy of thirteen had worked for three days without any food at all. The same boy complained that he had a drunken father, an improvident mother and had never owned a pair of shoes or stockings in his life.

An inquest held on 28 July 1856 into the death of twenty-nine-year-old Charles Dolling at the colliery states that the owner was by then a Mr Marsden. Dolling died when the pit face gave way, burying him and a boy. The boy was pulled free but Dolling suffocated.

Crown Colliery was acquired by Gabriel Goldney, an MP for Chippenham, in the early 1860s. In 1864 he donated a small plot of land to the Elders of St Barnabas church to be used to build a school for the impoverished in the locality, including the miners at his pit.

The Midland Railway opened their line to Bath in 1869. The route passed within feet of the colliery and the railway was forced to pay Goldney compensation in return for him not mining the coal beneath Warmley station.

In 1873 a tramway was proposed linking the pit to the railway, and Goldney asked the permission of the Kennet & Avon Canal Co. to remove a section of the Dramway so that his new tramway could cross their route. No objections were raised, with the K&ACC acknowledging that the Dramway hadn't been used for over twenty years. On 26 November 1879, Goldney again

approached the canal company, offering to buy the Dramway and all houses, cottages and land belonging to it for £1,200. His offer was declined.

The 1880 List of Mines states that the owner of the pit at that time was E.L. Owen. It is likely, however, that Mr Owen was leasing it from the Goldney family.

Crown Colliery closed in 1888 and over 100 people lost their jobs, although many found work at the nearby Cowhorn Hill Colliery. At the turn of the century, an attempt was made to reopen the pit and a new engine house and chimney were built in an attempt to drain it. Dawson's of Clutton erected the new smokestack in 1900, using specially curved bricks made at brickworks opposite the pit.

A drift mine was started at Webbs Heath with the intention of working the coal seams at both ends. Unfortunately, the shaft was driven at the wrong angle and in the wrong place, and the project was abandoned in January 1901. Several more attempts were made to open the pit but the Midland Railway refused to allow the coal under its railway to be worked, and none of the attempts succeeded.

The 1900 chimney stack at Crown Colliery survived until January 1981 when it was demolished at a cost of £1,489. The firm that demolished the stack was the same that built it, and the bricks were used as landfill in the clay pit of the same pottery that fired them.

One of the brickmakers was a local man called Jesse White. He scratched his name, and the names of his children, on many of the bricks before they were fired. After the demolition of the chimney several of his named bricks were saved. Two can be seen at the Bristol Industrial Museum and ten are in the Kingswood Museum collection.

100 Opposite: This building stands opposite the engine house and is thought to have been the blacksmith's workshop.

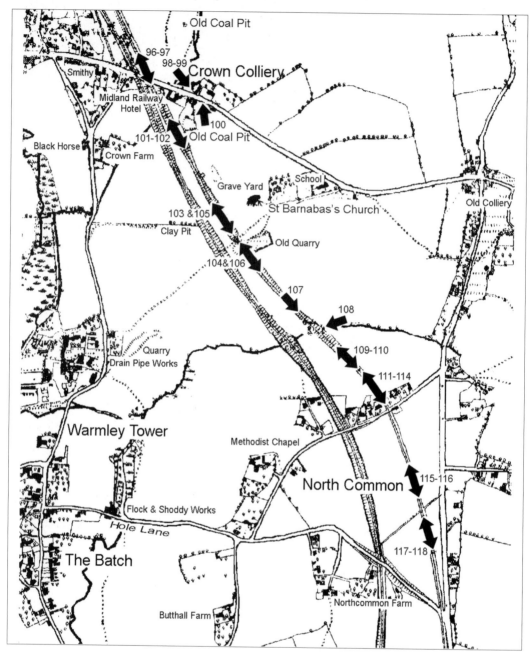

Old Coal Pit

96-97

98-99

Crown Colliery

Smithy

Midland Railway
Hotel

100

Black Horse

Old Coal Pit

101-102

Crown Farm

Grave Yard

School

St Barnabas's Church

Old Colliery

103 &105

Clay Pit

Old Quarry

104&106

107

108

Quarry
Drain Pipe Works

109-110

111-114

Warmley Tower

Methodist Chapel

Flock & Shoddy Works

Hole Lane

North Common

115-116

117-118

The Batch

Butthall Farm

Northcommon Farm

101 Opposite above: After a short detour around the back of a builder's yard, the original route of the Dramway is regained.

102 Opposite below: Looking south and the Dramway is now in a reasonably deep cutting. There was once a branch here that led to Crown Colliery. It took four weeks to build at a cost of £31 15s.

103 The route then passes under St Ivel Way, a footpath leading to St Barnabas church. The A&GR received a rent of *6d* every six months from the church for the use of its land for the path.

104 A view of the other side of the bridge.

105 Looking north from the bridge. After abandonment, this section of the Dramway suffered badly from flooding, and people using the route as a footpath would often find the ground underfoot waterlogged. In 1985 the area was recommended for a grant under the Shell Better Britain Campaign so that drainage work could be carried out.

106 The view south from St Ivel Way.

107 *Above:* Brunel Close in Warmley is built on the site of an old quarry. The stone blocks in the ground at this location mark the spot where a passing loop existed.

108 *Right:* The Dramway then crosses a small stream on a high embankment. During 1831 it suffered from subsidence and the stone sleepers were temporarily replaced with wooden ones to help spread the weight of the coal wagons passing along it.

109 This section of the Dramway ends at a wooden barrier.

110 The route then crosses Grassmere Gardens in North Common.

111 Between Grassmere Gardens and Windmere Way the Dramway route was deliberately left as a path while a housing estate grew up around it. It was originally going to have a tarmac surface; however, during preparatory work a section of stone sleeper blocks was discovered. The contractors were approached by the Bristol Industrial Archaeological Society and persuaded to surround the blocks with stone chippings instead.

112 Part of the Dramway has been swallowed up by a garden. The route is still visible by the inclusion of a marker through the lawn.

113 The route disappears for a short distance under new housing, before reappearing as a lane behind houses on Poplar Road.

114 On 19 April 1989, a Mr Bowell observed that contractors laying a new gas supply along Poplar Road had uncovered a section of Dramway rail. He telephoned Dave Sutton, the Kingswood Borough Council Conservation Officer, who in turn alerted Bristol Industrial Archaeological Society members to the discovery. The site was visited the following morning, and the contractors were persuaded not to cover it up until a rare double-chair, specifically designed to carry the Dramway across a road, had been saved. The chair and two sections of rail were removed and are now on display at the Kingswood Heritage Museum.

115 As the route approaches an industrial estate in North Common, sleeper blocks have been placed in a gravel path.

116 *Opposite above:* A view behind the industrial estate.

117 *Opposite below:* At Southway Drive an industrial unit has been erected upon the Dramway route.

118 A view looking north. The official Dramway footpath leaves the route here and takes a detour along the Bristol to Bath cycle path as far as Cherry Garden Lane.

Hole Lane and Bull Hall Collieries

Hole Lane (which also appears on maps and records spelt as Haul Lane) and Bull Hall collieries are thought to have been in operation since the early 1800s. The owner of the two pits and the nearby Cowhorn Hill Colliery was Robert Leonard Jefferies, proprietor of the Hole Lane Coal Co. All three pits were connected underground.

The early documented history of Hole Lane Pit is a catalogue of accidents. An inquest on 28 November 1809 tells how fifty-three-year-old John Batt was killed when the roof caved in on him. He left a wife and six children. John was buried in Siston on 4 January 1810.

Seventeen-year-old John Fray is mentioned in an inquest at Bitton on 4 August 1814. He was killed when a single stone fell on him, a ton in weight. An inquest at Bitton on 12 June 1815 tells how twenty-four-year-old Joseph Somerville was killed after falling down the pit shaft. In 1817 Samuel Harvey was killed by stone and coal falling on him. His inquest at Oldland Common was on 23 April 1817. Similarly, twenty-eight-year-old Isaac Bush was killed by rubbish falling on him in 1822. His inquest took place at Oldland on 9 March of that year.

In December 1830 Hole Lane Pit sent a load of coal along the Dramway to Keynsham. This was the first load of coal to traverse the then unfinished route. At that time the pit was not directly connected to the Dramway and the wagons were loaded on the mainline.

On 30 July 1831 an Act of Parliament was passed allowing the A&GR to build a branch from the Dramway to the pit at a length of 6 chains. This was completed by February 1832 at a cost of £80 17s 5d. The colliery had paid £55 for two wagons the previous December. In 1833 a 70ft-long shed at Londonderry Wharf was erected, for which the colliery paid the A&GR a rent of £20 per annum.

The 1841 Children's Employment Commission records show that the three pits worked by the Hole Lane Coal Co. employed about 150 people, forty who were under the age of thirteen and one who was seven but who had started working when he was six.

An interview with Mr Samuel Long, the forty-eight-year-old colliery under-manager at Hole Lane, states:

> The seams worked are 6ft and 2ft 6in while the depth of the shafts are 108, 60, and 34 fathoms and worked by steam-engines. The Cowhorn Pit requires sixteen hours out of twenty-four pumping to keep dry: the engine is thirty-six-horsepower.

Mr Long goes on to say that the pit was worked between the hours of 5 a.m. and 1 p.m. with a half-hour break for a meal. Maintenance work was carried out at night and this work usually involved repairing the roads and pit timbers. The boys who did this work were allowed to rest during the day and would work the nightshift every other week.

Most of the boys could read, some could write and most went to Sunday school. Any man or boy who was caught swearing had to pay a fine of 1s or 'quit the work'. The fine was paid into a sick fund which was supplemented by the earnings of the workers. Men and boys who earned 1s a day paid 2d a week to the fund, and those earning less than 1s paid 1d.

Work underground involved the larger boys pushing carriages that could carry 480lb of coal, while the smaller boys pushed carriages holding 240lb. Two boys would work each carriage. The larger boys would bring out the coal from the stalls by sliding on a wooden ladder up an incline of 2ft in every 12ft. The ladder was formed of a 16in plank laid on the floor with cross bars about 1ft apart. The boys would ascend this on their hands and feet, with tubs of coal following behind attached to a chain that passed between their legs. The chain itself was fixed to a girdle of rope around the waist. Each tub held 120lb of coal.

The interview with Mr. Long was carried out on 24 May 1841. It was reported that about ten days previously a man had been killed by a fall of a heading whilst 'hunching', i.e. cutting in underneath a coal seam. He was working without using props.

By 1867 the collieries along the Dramway were closing due to exhaustion and flooding, and Hole Lane Pit sent its last load of coal to the wharfs at Keynsham in January 1867. Despite this, the Midland Railway built a bridge to maintain the link with Bull Hall Colliery when it built its extension to Bath in 1869.

Bull Hall and Hole Lane have abandonment plans dated 1873, but both appear on the 1875 List of Mines under the ownership of Robert Jefferies. In 1876 they were bought, along with Cowhorn Hill Colliery, by Abraham Fussell, owner of the Oldland Colliery Co. and California Pit.

Hole Lane Colliery disappeared from the List of Mines in 1879 and Bull Hall is said to have been capped in 1881.

Oldland Common – Hole Lane Pit – Bull Hall Pit

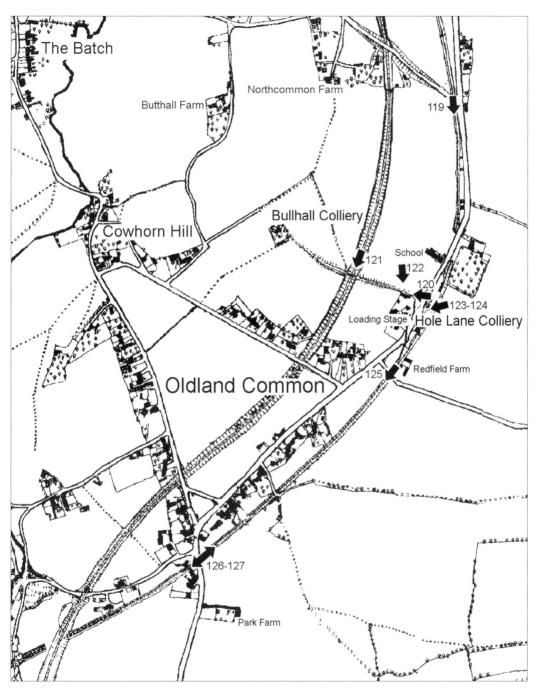

The Batch

Northcommon Farm

Butthall Farm

119

Bullhall Colliery

Cowhorn Hill

121

School

122

120

123-124

Loading Stage

Hole Lane Colliery

Oldland Common

125

Redfield Farm

126-127

Park Farm

119 After the trading estates in the last section we pick up the route of the Dramway at the junction of Victoria Road and High Street. This stretch of grass was once a cutting and the Dramway passed to the rear of the building in the distance, before passing under High Street in a sixty-six-yard-long tunnel.

120 This building on High Street is all that remains of Hole Lane Pit, the last colliery to send coal along the Dramway before its reopening to serve California Pit. There was a branch from here that went across the bridge in the distance (which straddled the Midland Railway's Mangotsfield–Bath main line) to Bull Hall Pit.

121 The Dramway bridge that led to Bull Hall Pit as viewed from the ex-Midland Railway route to Bath. The station behind it is Oldland Common on the Avon Valley Railway.

122 Another look at the surviving building. This was a blacksmith's shop.

123 This row of houses stands on the site of the pit.

124 The Dramway route through Oldland Common has been built upon, although various boundary walls give away the path it once took.

125 Looking south along the route of the Dramway at Redfield Hill. The route north of this spot was originally a cutting but it has been filled in and mostly built on. The Dramway passed under Redfield Hill in a short tunnel.

126 The route of the Dramway north from Barry Road is obvious. However, it would have been in a cutting at this spot and would have passed under the road in a tunnel.

127 The view south shows that the next section of Dramway has been filled in and built upon. This section had two tunnels. The first was seventy-three yards in length and unlined. The rock through which the tunnel passed was of sufficient strength that no sleeper blocks were needed; the rails were bolted directly to the tunnel floor. When the Midland Railway built its route to Bath it passed over the tunnel and a small section was brick-lined to increase its strength. The second tunnel was ten yards in length and passed under Cherry Garden Lane. Between the two tunnels was a 70–80ft-deep cutting that was filled in the 1960s.

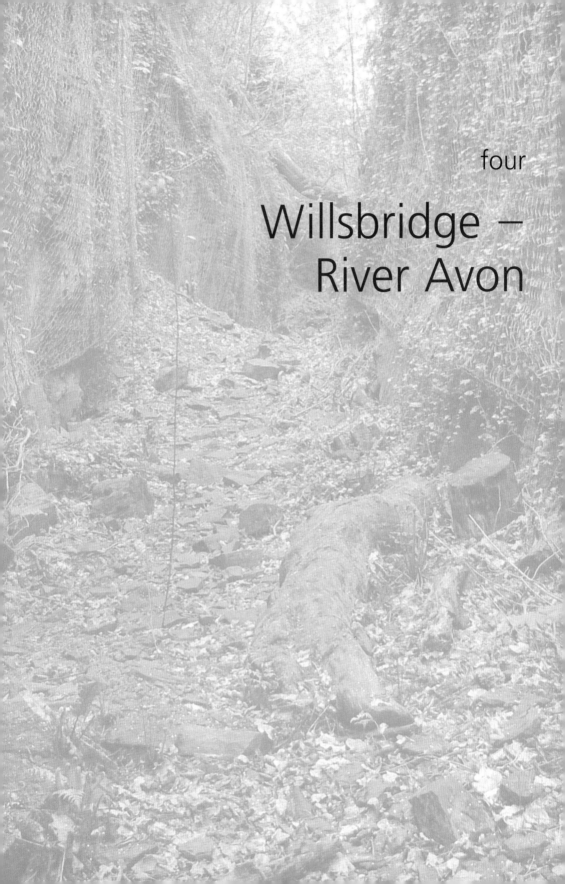

four

Willsbridge –
River Avon

California Colliery

128 California Colliery.

California Colliery was an old pit reopened in 1876 by fifty-one-year-old Abraham Fussell, owner of a shoe and boot manufacturing factory in Kingswood employing 100 workers. For this new venture he founded the Oldland Colliery Co. He deepened an old shaft to 522ft and renamed it California in the belief that, like the gold prospectors across the Atlantic, he was about to make his fortune. The main works were close to Oldland church, and there was a second shaft 474ft deep about half a mile north which provided ventilation. This, too, was an old pit reopened, and was previously known as Peg House.

Fussell modernised the colliery with a twin-cylinder winding engine, and five Lancashire boilers provided steam. The pumping engine was made locally by Gregory of Kingswood Hill. It was a direct-acting condensing engine with a 60in diameter cylinder and a 9ft stroke.

The pit was one of very few locally to use compressed air for cutting coal at the face and for powering the underground haulage engines. The compressor house contained a pair of horizontal air-compressing engines, each of which had steam cylinders of 21in diameter and air cylinders of 25in diameter. Iron pipes led from the compressor house to the second shaft and to Cowhorn Hill Colliery.

Needing a way to get his coal to the markets of Bristol, Fussell decided to connect his colliery with the by then derelict Dramway, which lay across Willsbridge Valley on the other side of Siston Brook. Undeterred by the terrain, a new branch of the Dramway was built and routed from the colliery down a 1-in-10 incline, across Siston Brook on a bridge, and connected via a new trailing junction with the main A&GR route. The junction was built in such a way that any runaways on the incline would be diverted uphill where they would come to a natural halt, rather than careering downhill out of control in the direction of Willsbridge.

The Dramway itself was repaired at the expense of the colliery, and a new land wharf was built at Willsbridge to supply local markets with California Colliery coal.

The necessary works required to reopen the Dramway were completed in 1881. The census of that year states that Fussell then employed over 500 hands, and that his sons George, Philip and Sidney were involved in his various businesses. The colliery had experienced problems with flooding due to the deepening of the pit which, combined with the expense of linking to the Dramway, meant the venture initially lost a great deal of money. However, by the end of the 1880s things had turned around and Fussell was offered £30,000 for the workings. He declined to sell.

Abraham Fussell died in 1887 at the age of sixty-two while having an operation to remove a tumour in his tongue. Four years later, the 1891 census listed his son Philip as the colliery owner, and George and Sidney as running the footwear factory. The same census showed twenty-four-year-old Frederick Charles Sadler as a boarder on a farm in Oldland. Mr Sadler had just become the colliery manager.

129 The remains of California Colliery have been converted into an attractive private dwelling.

The 1896 'List of Mines worked under the Coal Mines Regulation Act' verifies the manager of the pit as F.C. Sadler and names the under manager as Peter Lovell. 107 people worked underground, with an additional twenty workers on the surface. In 1898 Philip Fussell bought the rights to the mineral workings of New Pit Colliery and the Golden Valley Colliery from the Brain family to prevent competition. Philip was a connoisseur of the arts and filled the family home, Fair View House, with a considerable collection of paintings.

A tragic accident occurred at the pit in 1899 when fifty-two-year-old Charles Brain died after timbers holding up the roof gave way. The inquest was held at The White Hart Inn, Old Market on 27 May.

George Fussell died in 1900 at the age of fifty-three and Philip took over the management of the footwear factory with George's son, Harry, at his side. Sidney became the new owner of the colliery. The following year's census lists the colliery manager Frederick C. Sadler as being married with two children. His next-door neighbour was Charles Fussell, a fifty-eight-year-old miner from Siston. Peter Lovell, the under manager, was fifty-one and living near Tower Road in Warmley. His nineteen-year-old son Gilbert was an engine driver at the pit.

The colliery was worked until March 1904 when an inrush of water from old workings rapidly flooded the pit causing its closure and bankrupting the Oldland Colliery Co. 300 men lost their jobs. The site was acquired by West Gloucester Water Works who installed a steam pumping engine which extracted water from the pit until the late 1960s. One of the directors of the West Gloucester Water Works was Sidney Fussell.

The colliery manager Frederick Sadler is recorded in the 1908 'List of Mines' as working for Warmley Collieries Ltd at their Goldney Pit. He was in charge of fifty men below ground and ten above.

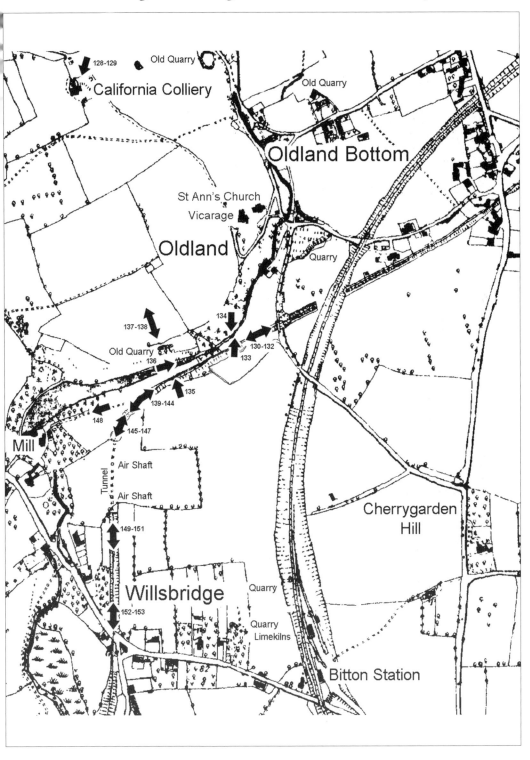

128-129

Old Quarry

California Colliery

Old Quarry

Oldland Bottom

St Ann's Church
Vicarage

Oldland

Quarry

137-138

134

Old Quarry
··· 136

130-132

133

135

139-144

148

145-147

Mill

Tunnel

Air Shaft

Air Shaft

149-151

Cherrygarden
Hill

Willsbridge

Quarry

152-153

Quarry
Limekilns

Bitton Station

130 The Dramway emerges from the ten-yard tunnel under Cherry Garden Lane. This is the view looking back towards the tunnel.

131 The bricked-up tunnel portal is just visible, although almost completely buried under earth and mud.

132 The official Dramway footpath rejoins the route south of this location. Unfortunately nothing points the casual observer to the tunnel's existence.

133 After exiting the tunnel the Dramway follows the route of Siston Brook on a 40ft-high embankment.

134 The view of the Dramway from Siston Brook. The harsh winter of 1831 was followed by a dry summer in 1832 which caused the embankment at this spot to become unstable. The subsidence was countered by the building of a 30ft high retaining wall. The material used came from piles of stone left on top of Willsbridge Tunnel during its construction.

135 The next four photographs show the remains of the incline that led from the Dramway to California Colliery. This is Tramway Junction, a triangular section of land at the foot of the incline.

136 The bridge across Siston Brook at the base of the incline as viewed from the bottom of the valley.

137 The incline is Grade II listed and was operated by gravity. Loaded wagons descending the incline pulled up empty ones. This is the view uphill.

138 Further up the hill the incline scours its way through the hillside with massive retaining walls on both sides.

139 Back on the Dramway itself, and closer to Willsbridge Mill, the council have marked the route with two markers and a sculpture.

140 The first item in the previous photograph is this lovely marker block.

141 The sculpture is made from Dramway sleeper blocks and has lumps of coal texturing the top surface. The rails are marked 'British Steel 2000'.

142 Left: The second marker shows that this section of the Dramway stands in the Willsbridge Mill local nature reserve.

143 Below: Slightly further south the route of the Dramway is sadly blocked by these imposing gates. Beyond here the Dramway passes through a deep cutting and Willsbridge tunnel. In 1935 the section of the Dramway between Willsbridge Hill and Cherry Garden Lane was sold to the West Gloucestershire Water Co., who used it to construct a water main from the flooded California Colliery to a valve chamber at Willsbridge.

144 Opposite above: The view north from the gates.

145 Opposite below: Willsbridge tunnel is approached via a dark and gloomy, sheer-sided and narrow cutting. The portal sits at the bottom of a 60ft-high ashlar block wall. The tunnel itself is 156 yards long, 8ft 6in high at the centre, 9ft 5in to 10ft wide at track level and brick-lined throughout.

146 *Above:* The view north from the tunnel portal. During the Second World War the tunnel was used as an air-raid shelter and was home to up to 500 people. It has two ventilation shafts which were covered to prevent light reaching enemy bombers. These ventilation shafts are unusual in that one is round and the other square. After the war the tunnel was used for a time as a mushroom farm.

147 *Below:* I poked the camera through a gap in the tunnel door and took this photograph. During its construction a mistake was found in its level and the contractor had to deepen it. The tunnel cost £49 17s to complete. The contractor spent £7 18s on gunpowder from a Mr W. Taylor, and a further £11 10s for gunpowder from a Mr C. Anthony.

148 Right: The official Dramway footpath skirts the hill and is routed through the grounds of Willsbridge Mill. Ironically, this was the route originally surveyed for the Dramway but, following objections from the mill's owner, John Winwood (who didn't want to be able to see the railway from his house), the Dramway was built with a deviation further up the hill.

149 Below: The south portal of the tunnel originally had flanking walls and a parapet, but these collapsed in the 1980s. The steel doors were installed in 1983 after a campaign by the Avon Wildlife Trust to better protect six species of bats living in the tunnel. The Trust paid for the grills which allowed the bats access and kept temperatures even.

150 Once again I poked the camera through a gap and got a shot of the interior. The tunnel has a bend at the northern end and it is not possible to see from one end to the other.

151 The view from Willsbridge Tunnel down to Willsbridge Hill. There was a 200ft-long passing loop here. Priority was always given to horses walking uphill rather than loaded drams making their way south.

152 Willsbridge Tunnel viewed from Willsbridge Hill. The route is on a very steep gradient here and, combined with its length, the horses that pulled the wagons must have really earned their livings.

153 The Dramway crossed the Hanham to Bath main road on the level. This is the 'Via Julia', the old Roman road from Bath to the river Severn. There were no crossing gates and residents were known to write to the local newspaper, complaining about the lack of warning before loaded wagons shot across the road.

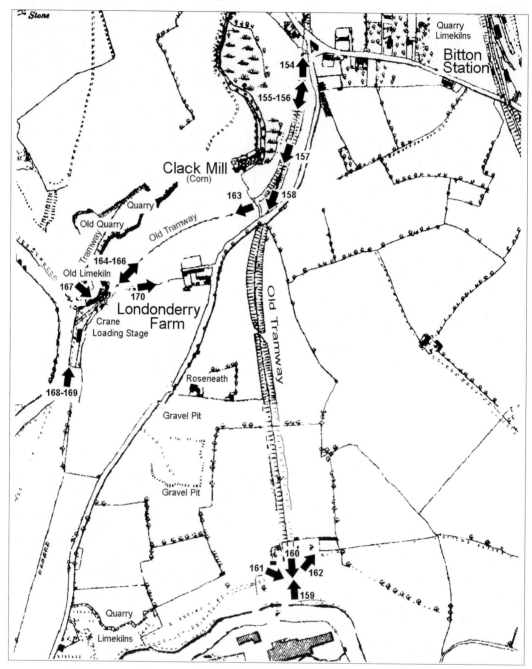

154 *Opposite above:* The building on the right was a weighbridge house for wagons destined for Willsbridge Wharf. It was built by the California Colliery.

155 *Opposite below:* The view north along Willsbridge Wharf. The weighbridge house has been extended across the trackbed.

156 Opposite above: Looking in the opposite direction to the previous image, this view looks towards the river Avon. In 1832 a siding was laid at the request of the Bristol Turnpike Trust and cost £21 1s 6d. When in use by the California Colliery, the wharf consisted of a 250ft-long passing loop and a 300ft-long siding.

157 Opposite below: The earthworks here show a V-junction which marks the start of the branch to Londonderry Wharf. Just visible on the left is the tunnel that took the Dramway route to Avon Wharf under the A4175 Keynsham Road.

158 Localised flooding, together with the style of architecture, often makes this 65ft-long brick-lined tunnel look like an abandoned canal. Beyond the A4175 the tunnel has been bricked up, and the cutting that was beyond it has been filled in and built upon.

Avon Wharf – The Backs

159 The Dramway terminus at Avon Wharf. The building on the left is Avon House and was the headquarters of the A&GR. It cost £179 16s 6d to build. The middle structure was a weighbridge house, and the Dramway passed between it and the workshop on the right before disappearing into a now filled-in cutting.

160 Looking towards the river Avon. The *Devizes and Wiltshire Gazette* of Thursday 7 November 1833 reported a fatal fight at the Backs between two men named Brown and Basset. The paper reported that the two men had been drinking together the previous Friday and had become very quarrelsome. Brown then proceeded to strike Basset in an attempt to get him to fight. After much provocation Basset agreed and, after sparring for a while, landed a blow which knocked Brown to the ground, killing him. An inquest took place before W. Joyner Ellis Esq. and Basset was committed to Gloucester prison on a charge of manslaughter.

161 The weighbridge house was fitted with a Foster, Rastrick & Co. weighing machine that was installed at the end of September 1830. This structure and Avon House are Grade II listed buildings. In the background is Kelston Round Hill, the site of prehistoric earthworks.

162 Other surviving structures at the Backs are a workshop-cum-mess room, and stables. Both these buildings are built from pennant stone, whereas the weighbridge house is built from Bath stone.

Londonderry Wharf

163 The branch to Londonderry Wharf crosses fields belonging to Londonderry Farm. In 1847 the A&GR agreed to pay £5 compensation to Dr Edwin Groves, who was leasing the farm and land at the Backs from the railway, for the 'foul state of the arable land'.

164 At the bottom of the field, and next to a kissing gate, Dramway rail has been reused to make a fence.

165 The view north across Londonderry Farm. During 1848 the route was repaired by a Mr David Wiltshire at a cost of £27 12s.

166 At the bottom of the field is an access road that leads from Londonderry Farm to the riverbank. Over 100 years have passed since the last train crossed this road, but stone sleeper blocks are still embedded in its surface.

167 The surviving stables and weighbridge house at Londonderry Wharf.

168 Standing on Londonderry Wharf looking north towards the spot where the Dramway entered the area.

169 The wharf had room to berth two coal barges at any one time.

170 The access road also has fencing made from recycled Dramway rail. Londonderry Farm is an ancient building. Records of 1666 tell of 'a roveless tenement' being bought by a Mr Richard Jones, who built a gentleman's residence on the property and named it Burnt House. This he sold to Thomas Coster, an MP for Bristol. In 1770 the house was bought by the K&ACC.

171 An artist's impression of a train on the Dramway.

five

The Dramway –
Operation

The Dramway was a horse and gravity railway. From Shortwood to the river Avon at Keynsham, the route descended 176ft in height over a length of 5 miles, 2 furlongs and 4 chains. The track consisted of cast-iron, fish-bellied rail that sat in chairs attached to stone sleeper blocks.

The horses walked between the rails on a coal ash path and a man accompanied the wagons ready to apply the brakes. All previously published records state that the men walked beside the wagons. I find this highly unlikely, for surely human nature is such that no one would walk 5 miles when there is a horse and cart to ride on. On the descent the horses would have had little to do, but on the ascent they would have worked hard, especially on the 1 in 76 section of line north of Willsbridge Road.

Each of the wagons on the Dramway held 4 tons of coal. They were painted with 2in-high characters which gave the name of the owning colliery, the identity number of the wagon, and its weight. Records published in April 1834 show that, in a five-day period, 243 tons of coal were shipped from Londonderry Wharf, and 1,025 tons of coal from Avonside. This equates to sixty-four wagons arriving at the southern end of the Dramway each day. This busy period in the Dramway's history helps explain the need for several 200ft-long passing loops along the route, and it is possible that horses worked in teams pulling several wagons along.

Wagons were originally purchased from Foster, Rastrick & Co., but the A&GR also built their own. An entry in the accounts book for February 1833 gives an interesting breakdown of materials used.

Wagons.

Bradley & Co for Wheels	£162 8s 9d
Ride & Parter for Sawing	£3
W. Harvey for Smiths	£3 15s
Wages	£18 14s 6d
Winwood & Co. for Castings	£3 17s 6d

Upon reaching the river Avon, wagons were weighed before the coal was unloaded onto barges. The cargo was then shipped to destinations along the river Avon or the Kennet & Avon Canal.

Storage was provided at Londonderry Wharf by the Coalpit Heath and Hole Lane collieries each building a 70ft-long shed. These were connected to the Dramway by two sidings. Another shed was built by the Shortwood Colliery. The wharf itself had room to berth two coal barges at any one time.

In 1832 the A&GR took delivery of an 86ft-long barge that was capable of holding 180 tons of coal carried in sixty boxes on two tiers. The barge was hired to the Coalpit Heath Co. for £320 per year. The boxes were transported from the pit to the barge on specially designed carriages, each carriage holding two 3-ton boxes. In April 1834 nineteen of these carriages were offered for sale, and were disposed of in 1835.

Tolls

The tolls on the A&GR were set at 2*d* per ton, per mile. Fractions were set at a quarter of a ton, and a quarter of a mile.

Storage Costs

The toll for the storage of all coal, culm, lime, lime-stone, clay, iron, iron-stone, iron-ore, lead-ore or any other ores, timber, stone, bricks, tiles, slate and gravel was set at 2*d* per ton.

2*d* was payable for the warehousing of every package not exceeding 56lb in weight, and 4*d* for packages weighing above 300lb, but not exceeding 600lb. Packages weighing over 1,000lb were stored at a cost of 6*d*.

Goods or other articles that remained on site longer than fourteen days had to pay a further sum of one penny per ton if stored in the open, and two-pence per ton if stored in a warehouse. This price was applied for the next three days after which the price incremented by a penny for every three days extra that the goods remained on site.

Cranage Rates

The lifting of any weight under 2 tons was charged at 6d per lift. Over 2 tons, but fewer than 3, cost 1s. Over 3 tons, but under 4, cost 1s 6d. Anything over 4 tons was charged at a further sixpence per ton.

California Colliery

Wagons used by California Colliery were painted dove grey and were left unlettered. The colliery owned twenty 4T tipping coal wagons with sloping ends, three 4T coal wagons and one 2T coal wagon. They were fitted with four wheel brakes.

A report in the *Bath Weekly Chronicle* of 9 June 1934 from a Mr Ham of Willsbridge recounts how wagons from the colliery would descend the line in pairs with a brakeman on each wagon. A boy would run in front of the train opening the various level-crossing gates. No horses were used on the descent but, once a sufficient number of wagons had been collected at Londonderry Wharf, a horse would take them back to the incline at Tramway Junction.

The accuracy of this report is unknown, and published histories of the line state that there were no level crossing gates at Willsbridge when the Dramway was built, and the route crossed no other major roads on the descent to the river. Of course, the colliery company may have installed gates on the roads when it rebuilt the line, although there is no evidence of this.

Acknowledgements

The biggest thanks for help with this book go to my wife and two daughters who have happily trudged through ankle-deep mud while I researched and photographed the remains of this amazing old artefact. I would also like to thank Cath for her help with research, and for proofreading the book for me. Her inspiration and help have both been invaluable.

A big thanks, also, to Clive Moore for his additional research, for being a sounding board, and for the use of his rather excellent photographs of the Dramway around Mangotsfield and Siston. Thanks mate, much appreciated! Thanks also go to Katie Thomas for the use of her Bristol Industrial Archaeological Society magazine articles, and all at the Kingswood Heritage Museum for kindly allowing me to photograph their exhibits.

Finally, I would like to extend my thanks to Mr Blyth W. Young and the staff of the Murco Westerleigh Oil Terminal for their enthusiastic help in obtaining photos of the Dramway route through their premises.

I would also like to express my gratitude to the following people for the use of their photographs:

Chris Hopkins: No.35.
Jenny Cornwell: Nos 44, 98, 128.
Clive Moore: Nos 49, 50, 51, 56, 57, 58, 59, 60, 63, 76, 78, 81, 82.
Mark Annand: Nos 65, 66, 67, 75.
Bristol Central Library: No.83.
Stephen Dowle: Nos 89, 94, 95.

Bibliography

Some books which have proved useful:

Coal and the Dramway (within rural Bitton), Ian S. Bishop.
History of Kingswood Forest, A Braine.
The Bristol and South Gloucestershire Coalfield, Peter Brown.
Children's Employment Commission Report. Elijah Waring.
The Bristol Coalfield, John Cornwell.
Colleries of Kingswood and South Gloucestershire, John Cornwell.
The Bristol & Gloucester Railway and the Avon & Gloucestershire Railway, Colin G. Maggs.
Priestley's Navigable Rivers and Canals 1831, Joseph Priestley.
The Bristol Coal Industry, Keith Ramsey.
'Discoveries in Polar Road'. *B.I.A.S. Journal*, Katie Thomas.

Thanks also go to the Bristol Record Office, the Bristol Central Library, the Gloucestershire Record Office and the National Archives at Kew.

Anyone in need of refreshment after visiting the remains of the Dramway should pay a visit to the excellent café at the Avon Valley Railway. Tea, cake and atmosphere like no other place in Bristol. Highly recommended.

www.bristol-rail.co.uk

Other titles published by Tempus

Bristol Transport
DAVID CHEESLEY

This well researched and informative book includes a collection of over 200 old photographs charting the history of transport in Bristol. David Cheesley has written a number of books on Bristol for Tempus.

0 7524 1083 0

Haunted Bristol
SUE LE QUEUX

This enthralling selection of newspaper reports and first-hand accounts recalls strange and spooky happenings in the city of Bristol. This unique account is sure to appeal to anyone interested in a spot of ghost-hunting.

0 7524 3300 8

The Bristol Aeroplane Co.
DEREK N. JAMES

This book chronicles the saga of the great aviation company which has occupied premises at Filton, near Bristol, for ninety years. Using illustrations and informative text, aviation author Derek James has created a valuable record of this company.

0 7524 1754 1

If you are interested in purchasing other books published by Tempus, or in case you have difficulty finding any Tempus books in your local bookshop, you can also place orders directly through our website
www.tempus-publishing.com